A check is a special piece of paper you use to pay someone instead of using cash. When you write a check, you're telling your bank to give money from your account to someone else. You fill in their name, the amount, and sign it. The person can take the check to their bank to get the money. It's like a promise to pay!

This Book belongs to:

Date

_____
Child's name

_____
Street Address

_____
City, State, Zip

Pay
To the order of   (Write your name here)

$ [   ]

(Fill in an amount like $1 or $100)

(Fill in an amount like "$1 of imagination" or "$100 of Adventures")

Dollars

Memo

(Write what this book means to you, like "For Fun Reading" or "For Learning About Money")

(Practice signing your name here!)

ISBN: 979-8-9870469-3-7
Printed in the United States of America

First Edition, August 2024

VENDIENDO CON MI GRANDPA

A Spanglish Story

Written By: Eliza M. Garza
Illustrated By: Isa Medina
Editor: Cris Ardis
Translator: Janet Escalera

Selling With My Grandpa

School is out for the summer, and I've been spending a lot of time at my abuelos' (**grandparents'**) house while my parents are at work. Every morning when I walk into their cozy home, I'm greeted by the delicious aroma of my abuelita's (**grandma's**) oatmeal with canela (**cinnamon**) and raisins (**pasas**). The sweet smell of the cinnamon sticks mix with the rich scent of my abuelito's (**grandpa's**) coffee brewing. It makes me feel right at home, filling the kitchen--and my heart--with happiness.

One of my favorite things to do is to watch my abuelito (**grandpa**) paint. Sometimes I pull up a chair and sit right beside him, looking closely. Other times I sit on his lap and get to watch each brush stroke up close! He learned oil painting by watching a man who has a show on television.

05

My grandpa draws all kinds of nice things, like mountains, trees, birds, rivers, and forests. He says it's called landscape art. My grandpa actually has customers who buy his paintings. He makes money selling his art!

ART FOR SALE!

"Grandpa, I want to learn how to make money (**dinero**) doing something I love, just like you, but I don't know how to paint. Do you have any ideas about what I can do?" says Carlitos.

"Abuelo, quiero aprender a ganar dinero como tú de algo que me guste hacer mucho, pero no sé pintar. ¿Tienes alguna idea de lo que puedo hacer?" dice Carlitos.

"Since you love raspas (**snow cones**) so much and it's hot outside, how about selling them? It's easy to get started, and we can make fun memories together!"

"Como te encantan las raspas y hace calor afuera, ¿Qué tal si las vendemos? Es fácil empezar, ¡y podemos crear recuerdos divertidos juntos!"

"Just like our friends, Lupita and Genaro! Yes, I would love to! How should we start?"

"¡Así como nuestros amigos Lupita y Genaro! ¡Sí, me encantaría! ¿Cómo podemos empezar?"

Well, first we need a

BUSINESS PLAN

This will act like a map to help guide us on our journey," Grandpa Chávez says.

"Bueno, primero necesitamos un plan de negocios.

Esto nos ayudará como un mapa para guiarnos," dice el Abuelo Chávez.

My grandpa says a **business plan** shows us what we need to do and helps us keep track of everything. We'll write down all the important details about our raspa stand, like what the name of it will be, where we'll set it up, and what flavors of raspas we'll sell. It will help us make our raspa stand the best it can be!

Business Plan

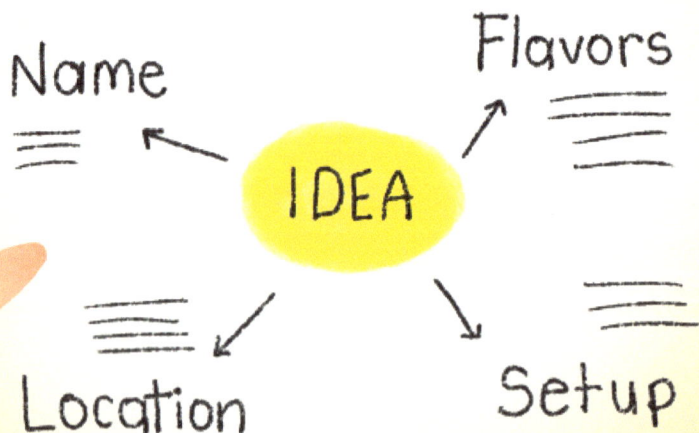

Name

Flavors

IDEA

Location

Setup

"Let's start with a fun and catchy name for your raspa stand," Grandpa says.

"Comencemos con un nombre divertido y que llame la atención para tu puesto de raspas", dice el abuelo.

"How about

"¿Qué tal

?"

"What a great name, Carlitos! Where do you want to sell them?"

"Me gusta mucho ese nombre Carlitos! ¿Dónde quieres venderlas?"

"Can we sell them in our front yard? I bet our neighbors would buy some!" Carlitos says.

"¿Podemos venderlas en la yarda? ¡Apuesto a que nuestros vecinos comprarían algunas!" dice Carlitos.

"Sure, but before we can start selling our raspas in the yard, we will need to go to City Hall to get a permit."

"Claro, pero antes de que podamos empezar a vender nuestras raspas en la yarda, necesitaremos ir al Ayuntamiento de la Ciudad para obtener un permiso."

"What's that?" Carlitos asks.   "¿Qué es eso?" pregunta Carlitos.

"It's like a permission slip from the city that shows it's OK for us to have our little business."

"Es como un permiso de la ciudad que dice que está bien que tengamos nuestro pequeño negocio."

CITY PERMIT

Name: _____

Permit # _____

"Sounds like a plan, Grandpa!"

"¡Suena como un buen plan, Abuelo!"

"Hop in the car. You can share all your great ideas on **products** and **pricing** on the way to City Hall."

"Sube al coche. Quiero que me compartas tus grandiosas ideas en productos y precios mientras vamos a la oficina del Ayuntamiento de la Ciudad."

On our way to City Hall, the place where we will receive the permit to sell our raspas, my grandpa says with a smile, "Before we start your raspa business, we need to figure out a few important things. First, we have to decide what flavors of raspas you want to sell."

En camino hacia el Ayuntamiento de la Ciudad, el lugar donde nos dan el permiso para vender nuestras raspas, con una sonrisa mi abuelo me dice, "Antes de comenzar tu negocio de raspas, necesitamos decidir algunas cosas importantes. Primero, tenemos que elegir qué sabores de raspas quieres vender."

15

"All of them!" Carlitos says, with wide eyes and using his outside voice.

"¡Todos!" dice Carlitos emocionado.

"You may want to keep it simple so you can make everything quickly and easily," Grandpa replies.

"Quizás quieras mantenerlo simple para poder hacer todo rápido y fácilmente", responde el abuelo.

"¡Oh! ¡Ya sé! (Oh! I know!) I'll have some of the most popular flavors - cherry, blue raspberry, strawberry, and pineapple. I'll include one of your favorites, too, Grandpa - tamarindo (**tamarind**)!" Carlitos says with a big grin on his face.

"¡Oh! ¡Ya sé! Voy a pedir algunos de los sabores más populares: cereza, frambuesa azul, fresa y piña. También voy a incluir uno de tus favoritos, abuelo - ¡tamarindo!" dice Carlitos con una gran sonrisa.

CHERRY

BLUE RASPBERRY

STRAWBERRY

PINEAPPLE

TAMARINDO

SUPER RASPAS

"Thank you, mijo. Will you have one size?" Grandpa asks.

"Gracias, mijo. ¿Vas a tener solo un tamaño?" el abuelo pregunta

"Yes, I think starting out with one size is best. Then, maybe, once I get the hang of this, I can add other sizes."

"Sí, creo que para empezar con un solo tamaño es lo mejor y luego, cuando le agarre el ritmo a esto, podré agregar otros tamaños."

17

"Eso (**That's it!**), Carlitos! This will help you serve your customers quickly. It's smart to start small and grow from there. You're already thinking like a real business owner! How much will you charge?"

"Eso Carlitos! Esto te ayudará a atender a tus clientes rápidamente. Es inteligente empezar pequeño e ir creciendo desde ahí. ¡Ya estás pensando como un verdadero dueño de negocio! ¿Cuánto vas a cobrar?"

"Since my raspas will be small, I would like to charge one dollar, Grandpa, but I think I need help figuring out the cost of my supplies first. I want to make sure there is enough money left over for me."

"Como mis raspas serán pequeñas, me gustaría cobrar un dólar, abuelo, pero creo que necesito ayuda para calcular los costos primero. Quiero asegurarme de que quede suficiente dinero para mí."

1

"Good job, mijo. The "leftover" money is called **profit**, and it's what you make after you pay for everything you need to run your raspa stand. First, we have our **total revenue**, which is all the money we make from selling raspas.

"Buen trabajo, mijo. Al "dinero que sobra" se llama ganancia y es lo que obtienes después de pagar todo lo que necesitas para operar tu puesto de raspas. Primero, tenemos nuestros ingresos totales, que es todo el dinero que ganamos vendiendo raspas.

TOTAL REVENUE

 =

2

Then we have our **expenses**, which are the costs of things like syrups, cups, and the permit.

Luego, tenemos nuestros gastos, que son los costos de cosas como jarabes, vasos y el permiso.

EXPENSES

When you subtract the expenses from the total revenue, the money left over is your profit."

Cuando restas los gastos de los ingresos totales, el dinero que queda es tu ganancia."

EXPENSES	GASTOS
− TOTAL REVENUE	− INGRESOS
= PROFIT	= GANANCIA

SYRUPS

CUPS

PERMIT

CITY PERMIT

Grandpa's eyes widen with excitement as he asks Carlitos, "Do you want to offer any special toppings like chamoy or gummy bears?"

Los ojos del abuelo se abren con emoción mientras me pregunta, "¿Quieres ofrecer algún ingrediente especial como chamoy o gomitas?"

"*yummm, yes!*"

Carlitos says imagining how delicious the raspas were going to be.

"¡Yummm, sí!" Carlitos dice imaginando lo deliciosas que van a ser los raspas.

SUPER RASPAS

SUPER RASPAS

20

"That's called an **upsell**, Carlitos, offering something extra to go with what a customer is already buying, to make it even better. It also helps you make more dinerito (**a little bit of money**) because the customer is buying more items from you."

"Eso se llama venta adicional, Carlitos, ofrecer algo extra a lo que el cliente ya está comprando para hacerlo aún mejor. También te ayuda a ganar más dinerito porque el cliente está comprando más cosas de ti."

"So I earn extra money on top of what they paid for the raspa?" asks Carlitos.

"Entonces gano dinero extra aparte de lo que ya pagaron por la raspa?" pregunta Carlitos.

"Exactly!"

"¡Exactamente!"

CITY HALL

When we arrive at City Hall, I notice it is a big building in the middle of our town. Grandpa says this is where the mayor and other people work to make sure everything in our city runs smoothly.

As we approach the information desk, my grandpa encourages me to ask the question myself. "Go ahead, mijo. Ask the receptionist what we need to know." Carlitos is a little nervous, but her smile helps put him at ease. "Hi, Ma'am. Where do we go to apply for a permit?"

Mientras nos acercamos al mostrador de información, mi abuelo me anima hacer la pregunta yo mismo. "Adelante, mijo. Pregúntale a la recepcionista lo que necesitamos saber." Carlitos está un poco nervioso, pero su sonrisa lo ayuda a sentirse tranquilo. "Hola señora. ¿A dónde vamos para solicitar un permiso?"

CITY HALL

She kindly replies, "The Permit Office is on the second floor. You can take the elevator down that hall to help you get there."

Ella responde amablemente, "La Oficina de Permisos está en el segundo piso. Puedes tomar el ascensor por el pasillo para llegar allí."

My grandpa and I ride the elevator to the second floor, fill out a form at the Permit Office, and pay a small fee. Now that we have our permit, we can set up our stand and start making raspas!

I don't have any money, and my grandpa already let me borrow $10.00 to pay for my permit, so I need to use the supplies we have at home.

As soon as we arrive home, I search through the cabinets. I find a blender to crush the ice, small disposable cups, spoons, straws, and a squeeze bottle for the syrup.

"Grandpa, how will I make syrup for the raspas?" Carlitos asks.

"Abuelo, ¿cómo voy a hacer el jarabe para las raspas?" pregunta Carlitos.

"We'll use Kool-Aid. It's simple and fun! I'll help you.

"Vamos a usar Kool-Aid. ¡Es sencillo y divertido! Te ayudo.

First, we need a packet of Kool-Aid powder in your favorite flavor.

Primero, necesitamos un sobre del polvo en tu sabor favorito.

1

Then, we mix the powder in a bowl with one cup of sugar.

Luego, mezclamos el polvo en un recipiente con una taza de azúcar.

2

Next, we pour one cup of water into the bowl with the powder and sugar and stir it really well until everything is dissolved.

Después, mezclamos una taza de agua en un recipiente con el polvo y el azúcar y revolvemos muy bien hasta que todo se disuelva.

3

4

TA-DA!

We have our very own homemade syrup for our raspas!"

¡Tenemos nuestro propio jarabe casero para nuestras raspas!"

Homemade
SYRUP

"Wow! That's cool!" Carlitos says.

"¡Wow, qué padre!" exclama Carlitos.

"Have you thought about making your raspa stand good for the environment?" Grandpa asks. "Practicing keeping our planet clean is called **sustainability**, and everyone can do it!"

"¿Has pensado en hacer que tu puesto de raspas sea bueno para el medio ambiente?" pregunta el abuelo. "La práctica para mantener nuestro planeta limpio se llama sustentabilidad ¡y todos podemos hacerlo!"

"I hadn't really thought about that, Grandpa. What if I commit to recycling all bottles and containers we use?" Carlitos asks.

"No lo había pensado mucho, abuelo. ¿Qué tal si me comprometo a reciclar todas las botellas y envases que usemos?" pregunta Carlitos.

"That's a great start! Don't worry if we don't have sustainable supplies this time around, mijo," Grandpa says reassuringly. "It's OK to start with what we have. Poco a poquito (**little by little**)."

"Claro, ¡es un gran comienzo! No te preocupes si no tenemos suministros sustentables esta vez, mijo", dijo el abuelo. "Está bien empezar con lo que tenemos. Poco a poquito."

"OK. I can do that!" Carlitos replies enthusiastically.

"¡De acuerdo, puedo hacer eso!" responde Carlitos entusiasmado.

"Should I make a bright and colorful sign to help people see my raspa stand, Grandpa? I think if we put it in the front yard, our neighbors and people driving by will want to buy from us!" suggests Carlitos.

"¿Debería hacer un letrero brillante y colorido para ayudar a la gente a saber de mi puesto de raspas, abuelo? Creo que si lo colocamos en la yarda, nuestros vecinos y las personas que pasan en auto querrán comprarnos," sugiere Carlitos.

"Excellent idea, Carlitos. That's called **advertising**! It's how we let people know we have something really great they should try. You may even want to add a **slogan**, a short, fun phrase that helps people remember your raspa stand."

"Excelente idea, Carlitos. ¡Eso se llama publicidad! Es cómo logramos que la gente se entere que tenemos algo realmente genial que deberían probar. Incluso podrías añadir un eslogan, una frase corta y divertida que ayude a la gente a recordar tu puesto de raspas."

SUPER RASPAS

Beat the heat with a TASTY TREAT!

Only $1 each!

"I got it! It will read in bold, colorful letters: 'Super Raspas - Beat the heat with a tasty treat! Raspas only $1 each!'" exclaims Carlitos.

"¡Lo tengo! Dirá en letras llamativas y coloridas: '¡Super Raspas! - ¡Combate el calor con un delicioso antojo! ¡Raspas solo $1 cada una!'" exclama Carlitos.

It's the perfect kind of weather for selling and eating raspas - hot! Setting up his stand in his grandpa's front yard is exciting! Grandpa says this part is called **operations**.

First, we unfold a small table and cover it with a bright yellow tablecloth.

I decorate the edges of the table with a colorful papel picado (**cut paper**) banner I made a couple of weeks ago while making arts and crafts with my Grandma Chávez.

Grandpa places the blender in the center, plugging it into the nearby outlet. Next, Carlitos arranges bottles of homemade syrup in different flavors on one side, along with stacks of cups, spoons, and some napkins. He even finds an old shoe box to use as a cash register to keep the money from flying away. Then his grandpa stakes an umbrella by the stand to help create some shade. Finally, Carlitos cleans and fills an old ice chest from the garage with cubed ice from Grandpa's freezer. Last, but not least, Carlitos hangs his homemade sign for all to see! Before he knows it, the first customers of the day line up!

SUPER RASPAS

Beat the heat with a TASTY TREAT!

Only $1 each!

Grandpa kneels beside Carlitos and says, "When someone comes up, welcome them with that big smile of yours. **Customer service** means being friendly and helpful. Be polite and listen to what they want. If they have questions, answer them as best as you can. And don't forget to thank them after they buy a raspa. Kindness will make your customers want to come again!"

El abuelo se arrodilla junto a Carlitos y dice: "Cuando alguien se acerque, recíbelos con esa gran sonrisa tuya. El servicio al cliente significa ser amable y servicial. Sé educado y escucha lo que quieren. Si tienen preguntas, respondelas lo mejor que puedas. Y no te olvides de agradecerles después de que compren su raspa. ¡La amabilidad hará que tus clientes quieran volver!"

Carlitos nods, eager to try out his new skills with his customers as he stands proudly behind his raspa stand. The sun beats down as Grandpa Chávez's longtime neighbors, Alonzo and Dolores, and their grandchild, Mandito, approach with smiles on their faces.

"Hola, Vecinos! (**Hi, Neighbors!**) How can I help you today?" Carlitos politely asks, while practicing his Spanish.

"**¡Hola, Vecinos! ¿En qué puedo ayudarte hoy?" pregunta Carlitos educadamente mientras practica su español.**

Dolores replies, "Hola, Mijo! (**Hi, My Son!**) Your raspa stand looks so inviting! We'd love to try your treats!"

Dolores responde, "¡Hola, Mijo, Tu puesto de raspas se ve tan atractivo! ¡Nos encantaría probar tus delicias!"

Before Carlitos can even say thank you, Mandito exclaims, "I want a rainbow raspa, please!"

Antes de que Carlitos pueda decir gracias, Mandito exclama: "¡Quiero una raspa arcoíris, por favor!"

SUPER RASPAS
Beat the heat with a TASTY TREAT!
Only $1 each!

"You got it! What can I make for you today, Mr. Alonzo and Ms. Dolores?"

"¡Claro! ¿Qué les preparar el día de hoy Señor Alonzo y Señora Dolores?"

We'll take a cherry and a blue raspberry."

"Nos llevaremos una de cereza y una de frambuesa azul."

Would you like to add any chamoy or gummy bears? Toppings are only 25 cents each." Carlitos asks, remembering to upsell like Grandpa taught him.

"¿Les gustaría agregar chamoy o gomitas? Los ingredientes extras cuestan solo 25 centavos cada uno," pregunta Carlitos, recordando ofrecer ventas adicionales como le enseñó su abuelo.

"Ooof! Que sabroso. (**How delicious!**) Please add both to mine," says Alonzo.

"Ooof! Que sabroso. Por favor agregalo al mío," dice Alonzo.

TOPPINGS

CHAMOY GUMMY BEARS

$.25 ¢ each!

37

"Sure. That will be $3.50 (three dollars and fifty cents)," Carlitos says.

"Claro. Serán $3.50 (tres dólares con cincuenta centavos)," dice Carlitos.

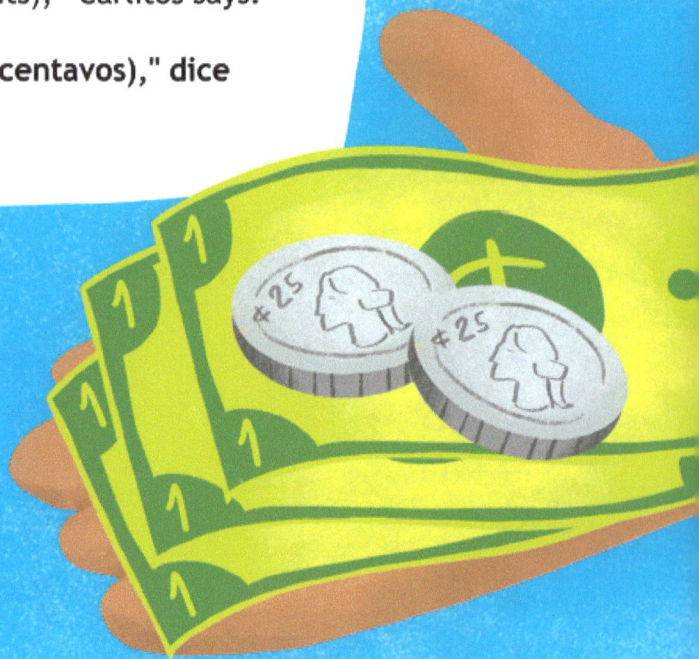

¿Necesitas ayuda, hijo?

Do you need help, Son?

Yes please, Grandpa. Can you please take the payment while I make the raspas (**snow cones**)?"

"Sí, por favor, abuelo. ¿Puedes encargarte del pago mientras preparo las raspas?"

"Claro."

"Of course."

Grandpa Chávez helps take the payment while Carlitos quickly puts on gloves to protect the items he is about to make from germs.

Cleanliness is always important when handling food so customers don't get sick!

Carlitos happily makes the raspas, covering every inch of ice with color and then hands the ice-cold treats to his neighbors with a satisfied look on his face.

Carlitos can't wait for them to take the first bite!

"Yummy!! This is the best raspa I've ever had," says Mandito as he jumps up and down.

"¡Yummy! Esta es la mejor raspa que he probado," dice Mandito mientras salta de alegría.

"These raspas really are super! You sure know what you're doing, Carlitos," Alonzo says.

"Están super estas raspas de verdad. Realmente sabes lo que estás haciendo, Carlitos," dice Alonzo.

Carlitos beams with joy. "I'm happy you like it! Thank you so much for stopping by. I hope you come again!"

Carlitos irradia alegría. "¡Me alegra que les haya gustado! ¡Muchas gracias por pasar por aquí! ¡Espero que vuelvan pronto!"

"We sure will. We'll make sure to share the good news with our friends so they can come out and support your business, too," says Dolores.

"Claro que sí. Nos aseguraremos de contarles a nuestros amigos para que vengan a apoyar tu negocio," dice Dolores.

Word got around fast! There is a long line of excited customers on the sidewalk in front of Grandpa Chávez's house most of the day. Everyone loves Super Raspas!

Carlitos says in amazement, "Grandpa, look! I sold out of all the raspas! I made so much money! I even have enough to pay back the $10 you let me borrow for my permit."

Carlitos dice asombrado: ¡Abuelo, mira! ¡Vendí todas las raspas! ¡Gané mucho dinero! Incluso tengo suficiente para devolverte los $10 que me prestaste para el permiso.

Grandpa Chávez smiles lovingly, watching Carlitos' excitement with pride.

"I'm so proud of you, mijo. You earned it. You worked hard and made people happy with your delicious raspas."

"Estoy muy orgulloso de ti, mijo. Te lo has ganado. Trabajaste duro e hiciste feliz a la gente con tus deliciosas raspas."

"What should I do with all this money, Grandpa?"

¿Qué debería hacer con todo este dinero, abuelo?"

Grandpa Chávez gestures to Carlitos to follow him to the front steps of his house. He sits down beside Carlitos, placing a gentle hand on his knee.

"El dinero, mijo, es pa' usarlo en muchas cosas diferentes. (**Money can be used for different things.**) It is a tool the world uses to buy things we need and want.

"**El dinero mijo, es pa' que se puede usar en diferentes cosas. Es una herramienta que el mundo utiliza para comprar cosas que necesitamos y queremos.**

BANK ACCOUNT

0123 4567 8910 1234

Money can be in the form of coins, paper bills, or even numbers on a card or in a bank.

El dinero puede estar en forma de monedas, billetes de papel o incluso números en una tarjeta o en un banco.

You could use it to learn something new, like taking a class or buying more supplies for your raspa stand."

Podrías usarlo para aprender algo nuevo, como tomar una clase o comprar más suministros para tu puesto de raspas."

44

"It's also important to save for something special you may need or want in the future. Do you know what a **bank** is?"

"También es importante ahorrar para algo especial que puedas necesitar o desear en el futuro. ¿Sabes qué es un banco?"

Carlitos shakes his head. "No, Grandpa."

Carlitos mueve la cabeza, "No, abuelo."

45

"A bank is a safe place where you can keep your money. They help give you the right ingredients to make your financial future as sweet as your favorite treat!."

"Un banco es un lugar seguro donde puedes guardar tu dinero. Te ayudan a tener los ingredientes adecuados para hacer que tu futuro financiero sea tan dulce como tu antojo favorito."

"Sounds interesting! How do they do that?"

"¡Suena interesante! ¿Cómo lo hacen?"

"Well, one of the ingredients is

SAVING

They help you save your money so you can use it later for important things.

"Bueno, uno de los ingredientes es el ahorro. Te ayudan a guardar tu dinero para que lo puedas usar más tarde en cosas importantes.

A **checking account** and a **savings account** are like special places to keep your money safe and organized at the bank.

Una cuenta de cheques y una cuenta de ahorros son como lugares especiales para mantener tu dinero seguro y organizado en el banco.

In a savings account, you put money aside for things you want in the future, like a new toy or something big, like a bicycle. It's like having a piggy bank at the bank!"

En una cuenta de ahorros, guardas dinero para cosas que quieres en el futuro, como un juguete nuevo o para algo grande como una bicicleta. Es como tener una alcancía en el banco."

CHECKING ACCOUNT

"A **checking account** is different because you use it for everyday things, like buying food or paying for fun things to do.

"Una cuenta de cheques es diferente porque la usas para cosas cotidianas, como comprar comida o pagar por cosas divertidas que hagas.

checkbook

NAME:
NUMBER:

$

Both accounts help you learn about managing money and keeping track of how much you have. It's a great way to learn how to save and spend wisely!"

Ambas cuentas te ayudan a aprender a manejar el dinero y a llevar un registro de cuánto tienes. Es una excelente manera de aprender a ahorrar y gastar de manera inteligente."

BANK ACCOUNT

567 8910 234
28

"That's cool, Grandpa!"

"¡Qué padre, abuelito!"

"That's not all, though. Banks also help your money grow by giving you a little extra money called **interest**. They can also **lend** you money if you promise to return it later.

"Eso no es todo, sin embargo. Los bancos también ayudan a que tu dinero crezca dándote un poco más de dinero llamado interés. También pueden hacerte un préstamo de dinero, si prometes devolverlo más tarde.

And if you're good at borrowing money and paying it back on time, you earn a score that's called **credit**. And just like that, you have the ingredients for a successful future for your money."

Si eres bueno pagando el dinero que se te prestó a tiempo, ganas una puntuación que se llama crédito. Y así, tienes los ingredientes para un futuro exitoso con tu dinero."

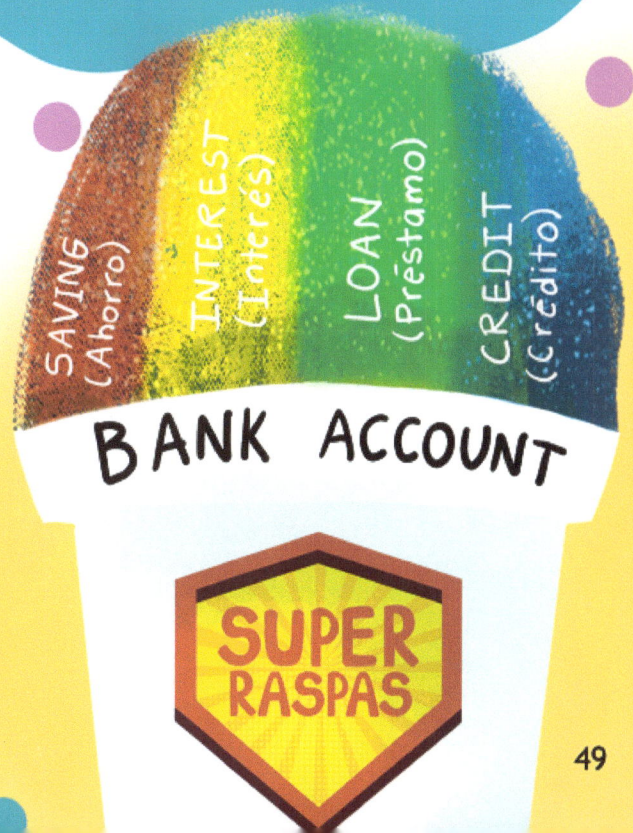

SAVING (Ahorro)

INTEREST (Interés)

LOAN (Préstamo)

CREDIT (Crédito)

BANK ACCOUNT

SUPER RASPAS

"Oh, I get it. So the bank keeps my money safe, gives me more money, and lets me borrow money?" asks Carlitos, paying close attention to his grandpa.

"Oh, ya entendí. Entonces, el banco guarda mi dinero seguro, me da más dinero y me da préstamos de dinero?" pregunta Carlitos, prestando mucha atención a su abuelo.

"Correct!"   "¡Correcto!"

"That sounds like a smart thing to do. I would like a piggy bank at the bank! I want to open a checking and savings account. Can we go now?"

Eso suena como algo inteligente. ¡Quiero una alcancía en el banco! Quiero abrir una cuenta de cheques y una cuenta de ahorros para mi dinero. ¿Podemos ir ahora?"

"Yes, of course! Listo, Mijo? (**Ready, Son?**)" Grandpa Chávez says as he gets up from the steps of his humble home.

"¡Claro que sí! ¿Listo, Mijo? El Abuelo Chávez pregunta mientras se para de estar sentado en las escaleras de su humilde casa."

Carlitos nods eagerly, clutching the money he made from his successful day and putting it in his pocket.

Carlitos mueve la cabeza con aceptación mientras aprieta los billetes metiéndolos en su bolsillo.

51

"Thank you for all your help, Grandpa. I could have never done this without you."

"Gracias por toda tu ayuda, Abuelo. Nunca habría podido hacer esto sin ti."

Abuelito pats Carlitos on the back gently as they walk toward the car, the South Texas heat still lingering in the air.

"De nada, Mijo. (**You're welcome, Son.**) I'm proud of how responsible and eager to learn you are. Remember, learning about money is just one part of growing up. Being kind and helping others, eso también es muy importante (**that is also very important**)."

"De nada, mijo. Estoy orgulloso de lo responsable y tenaz que eres para aprender. Recuerda, aprender sobre el dinero es solo una parte de crecer. Ser amable y ayudar a los demás, eso también es muy importante."

Carlitos grins, feeling grateful that his abuelito's guidance will always be with him, no matter what adventures come next.

Carlitos sonríe sintiéndose afortunado de que las enseñanzas de su abuelito lo acompañaran siempre, en todas las aventuras que lo esperan.

VENDIENDO CON MI GRANDPA
SPAN(GL)ISH GLOSSARY

#

¡Oh! ¡Ya sé! - (Oh! I know!)

A

Abuelita's - (Grandma's)
Abuelito's - (Grandpa's)
Abuelos' - (Grandparents')
Advertising - (Publicidad)

B

Bank - (Banco)
Business plan - (Plan de negocios)

C

Canela - (Cinnamon)
Checking Account - (Cuenta de Cheques)
Cleanliness - (Limpieza)
Credit - (Crédito)
Customer service - (El servicio al cliente)

D

Delicious - (Sabroso)
Dinero - (Money)

E

Eso - (That's it!)
Expenses - (Gastos)

I

Interest - (Interés)

L

Loan/Lend - (Préstamo)

M

Money - (Dinero)

N

Neighbors - (Vecinos)

O

Operations - (Operaciones)

P

Papel picado - (Cut paper)
Permit - (Permiso)
Poco a poquito - (Little by little)
Pricing - (Precios)
Products - (Productos)
Profit - (Ganancia)

R

Raisins - (Pasas)
Raspas - (Snow cones)

S

Saving - (Ahorro)
Savings Account - (Cuenta de Ahorros)
Slogan - (Eslogan)
Sustainability - (Sustentabilidad)

T

Tamarindo - (Tamarind)
Total Revenue - (Ingresos Totales)

U

Upsell - (Venta Adicional)

Y

Yarda - (Spanglish for Yard)
(Patio delantero Spanish for yard)
You're welcome - (De nada)

UNDERSTANDING YOUR DOLLAR

Did you know that a single dollar can be broken down into smaller parts? Let's explore how!

1 Dollar = 100 Cents!

A dollar is made up of 100 cents, and those cents come in different coins that you use every day.

Meet the Coins:

1. Penny
Value: 1 Cent
How many in a Dollar? 100 Pennies = 1 Dollar
Fun Fact: It's the only coin that's copper-colored!

2. Nickel
Value: 5 Cents
How many in a Dollar? 20 Nickels = 1 Dollar
Fun Fact: A nickel is bigger than a penny but worth more!

3. Dime
Value: 10 Cents
How many in a Dollar? 10 Dimes = 1 Dollar
Fun Fact: The dime is the smallest coin, but don't let its size fool you - it's worth 10 cents!

4. Quarter
Value: 25 Cents
How many in a Dollar? 4 Quarters = 1 Dollar
Fun Fact: Four quarters make up a whole dollar. You'll need quarters to use in vending machines or parking meters!

Putting It All Together:

You can make a dollar in so many different ways! Here are a few examples:
10 Dimes = 1 Dollar
4 Quarters = 1 Dollar
20 Nickels = 1 Dollar
100 Pennies = 1 Dollar
2 Quarters + 5 Dimes = 1 Dollar

Think About It!

- What could you buy with your dollar?
- How many different ways can you make a dollar with the coins you have?

Remember, every dollar counts! Learning how to use your coins wisely is the first step to becoming a smart saver and spender.

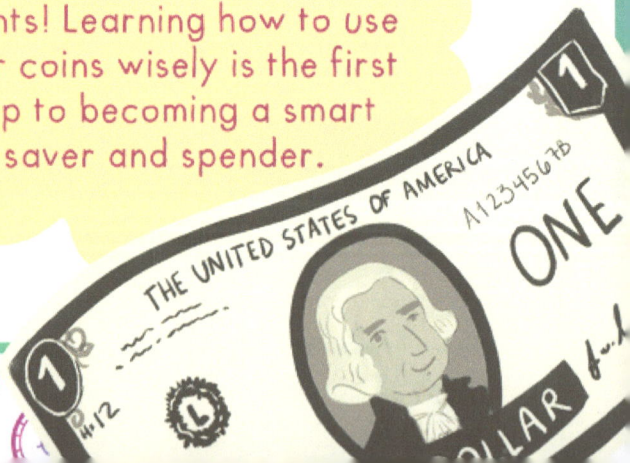

MONEY AROUND THE WORLD WORKSHEET

1. Match the Currency!

Draw a line to match the country with its correct currency.

Country	Currency
1. United States	A. Yen
2. Mexico	B. Euro
3. Japan	C. Dollar
4. European Union	D. Peso
5. United Kingdom	E. Pound

1. Color the Money!

Below are pictures of money from different countries. Color them in!.

1. Dollar Bill (USA):
   - Color it green and white.

2. Peso Coin (Mexico):
   - Color it gold and silver.

3. Euro Bill (European Union):
   - Color it with shades of blue and yellow.

4. Yen Coin (Japan):
   - Color it silver.

5. Pound Note (United Kingdom):
   - Color it purple and white.

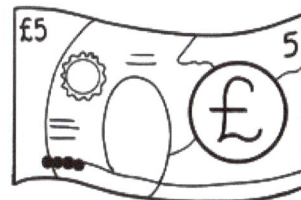

MEET THE REAL GRANDPA CHÁVEZ

This is Feliberto. He is remembered for being a fun, loving, and humorous grandpa that loved his wife, children, grandchildren deeply. He enjoyed having breakfast at Lee's Pharmacy in McAllen, TX, with his children and long-time friends. He enjoyed watching western movies, listening to music, cracking jokes, exercising, shopping, studying geography, writing poetry, painting, and reading his Bible. He really was always the first car in the pick-up line!

AUTHOR BIO

Eliza M. Garza is an Amazon best-selling, international award-winning author, resilience speaker, and entrepreneur from South Texas. She is passionate about her Hispanic heritage and believes that part of a child's pathway to empowerment and authenticity is understanding, identifying, and embracing their culture at a young age.

She is the founder of Adventure in a Cup, a program that provides children with the opportunity to learn the principles of entrepreneurship, financial literacy, and goal setting by running their own raspa stand for a day. Eliza was honored with a proclamation by her hometown, the City of McAllen, declaring a day in recognition of her work—Raspas Con Mi Grandpa Day. Eliza's book, Raspas Con Mi Grandpa, won the International Latino Book Award in the category of Best Educational Picture Book.

Eliza enjoys spending time with her family, which includes her spoiled poodle named Brinkley and a black cat named Holly. She also loves being an active member of her community and hosts collaborative and empowering events in her spare time.

BOOKINGS:

Book Eliza M. Garza for your next school function, book fair, conference, or corporate event.

E-mail:
authorelizamgarza@gmail.com
for more information.

Isa Medina is a mom, wife and an illustrator who lives in Mexicali B.C. She has illustrated several books throughout her career, working with publishers and independent authors from the U.S.A, Mexico, and Spain. In addition, she loves coffee, reading and spending time with her family, including her cat, Citripio.

JOIN OUR SUBSCRIBER LIST!

Subscribe to receive a free worksheet that extends the learning journey at home or in the classroom! Don't miss out on this valuable resource to keep the lessons going and make learning fun and engaging. Also, be the first to know about new book launches, book signings, special promotions, sales, giveaways, and more!

@authorelizamgarza

@authorelizamg

SCAN ME

FLOWCODE
PRIVACY.FLOWCODE.COM

TO UNLOCK MORE

www.ingramcontent.com/pod-product-compliance
Lightning Source LLC
Chambersburg PA
CBHW052054190326
41519CB00002BA/214